RACH

With Thanks

counting every blessing from God

BIBLE READING PLAN & JOURNAL

WITH THANKS
Bible Reading Plan and Journal
PUBLISHED BY RACHEL WOJO
Copyright © 2017 by Rachel Wojnarowski

Visit **www.rachelwojo.com/shop**

Requests for information should be addressed to rachel@rachelwojo.com

Trade Paperback

ISBN-13: 978-0692973721 (Rachel Wojo LLC)

ISBN-10: 0692973729

Cover design by Rachel Wojnarowski

Photo credit: Bigstock.com

All rights reserved. No part of this book may be reproduced, stored in a retrieval system or transmitted in any form or by any means, electronic or mechanical, including photocopying and recording, or by any information storage and retrieval system, without permission in writing from the publisher.

Library of Congress Cataloging-in-Publication Data

Printed in the United States of America
2017—First Edition--1001

Table of Contents

	Intro: With Thanks
	A Personal Note from Rachel
Day 1	1 Chronicles 16:1-8
Day 2	Psalm 7:10-17
Day 3	Philippians 4:1-7
Day 4	Psalm 9:1-9
Day 5	Psalm 145:1-10
Day 6	Psalm 105:1-7
Day 7	Psalm 95:1-6
Day 8	Psalm 136:1-9
Day 9	Ephesians 5:15-21
Day 10	Psalm 107:1-9
Day 11	Psalm 107:10-21
Day 12	Psalm 107:22-31
Day 13	Psalm 100:1-5
Day 14	1 Timothy 4:1-5
Day 15	Colossians 3:12-17

Table of Contents

Day 16	Isaiah 12:1-6
Day 17	Psalm 69:29-34
Day 18	Psalm 147:1-7
Day 19	Colossians 4:1-6
Day 20	Psalm 75:1-7
Day 21	Psalm 30:1-12
Day 22	Psalm 116:14-19
Day 23	1 Chronicles 16:27-34
Day 24	Psalm 26:1-7
Day 25	Psalm 28:1-7
Day 26	Hebrews 12:22-29
Day 27	1 Thessalonians 5:12-17
Day 28	Jeremiah 33:1-11
Day 29	Psalm 106:1-5
Day 30	Psalm 28:1-7
Day 31	2 Corinthians 9:6-15

A Personal Note from Rachel

Dear Friend,

Thank you for beginning this wonderful journaling experience through God's Word. My goal through Bible reading is to draw closer to Jesus, and I want that for you too!

Through reading daily Bible passages, praying, and listening to God, we're going to nurture and grow our relationship with him. This Bible reading plan and journal is specifically focused on counting every blessing from God with a thankful heart.

In a society that exhibits more and more self-centeredness each day, we can easily fail to be thankful for all that we have been given. Even when scarcity exists, the power in gratitude must not be overlooked. This Bible reading plan will help us recognize that sowing seeds of contentment will yield fruits of joy.

I'm thrilled to have you joining me! I pray you find the journaling section to be the perfect space for your individual needs.

Rachel

Counting Every Blessing from God

Welcome to the With Thanks Bible Reading Plan and Journal. I'm so excited to begin this journey with you! For the next thirty-one days, we are going to dig into God's word and grow closer to Him. Together we'll decide to forget what we don't have and focus on what we do.

> Joy is a gift that can't be held in your hand.
> *--One More Step*

Are you ready to give thanks for beyond what's tangible? You can share what you are learning on social media by using the hashtags #withthanksjournal and #biblereadingplan. Or you can just keep it between you and God.

4 Simple Steps to growing in faith

Step 1:
Pray: Spend some time with God in prayer. Prayer is simply having a conversation with him.

Step 2:
Read the Bible passage for the day one time slowly, soaking in each phrase. Read again if time allows.

Step 3:
Answer the daily question.

Step 4:
Complete the journaling section.

With Thanks

And they brought in the ark of God and set it inside the tent that David had pitched for it, and they offered burnt offerings and peace offerings before God. And when David had finished offering the burnt offerings and the peace offerings, he blessed the people in the name of the Lord and distributed to all Israel, both men and women, to each a loaf of bread, a portion of meat, and a cake of raisins. Then he appointed some of the Levites as ministers before the ark of the Lord, to invoke, to thank, and to praise the Lord, the God of Israel.
1 Chronicles 16:1-4

King David longed to restore the ark of the covenant to its rightful place within Israel. The ark had been created as a place for the Lord's presence to reside among his people. After being tossed around from city to city by the enemies, the ark rested in the city of Kiriath-Jearim, about 9 miles north of Jerusalem. David longed for the presence of the Lord to return to his people so he pitched a tent and called for the Levites to bring the ark back to Jerusalem. The ark was returned to the city and all the people rejoiced.

Seems like all should be good, right? David did his part of following the Lord's commands in how the ark was to be cared for. He brought it back to its rightful place. Surely, he did his duty. But David went a step beyond and assigned specific jobs to the Levites, the people God had appointed to care for the ark. I can hear the street talk now.

"I heard the ark is back in Jerusalem. Did you know they are hiring Levites?" "Yeah, I actually put in my application and I already received a position. I'm in the thanks and praise department."

I love that David believed thanksgiving and praise to the Lord was so very important that he appointed them as special duties to the Levites. Would you or I have enough experience to apply? Let's get it!

1 Chronicles 16:1-8

Day 1

Thankful

My praise and thanksgiving is important to God.

Confess and replace. What is in my heart that prevents me from being grateful to God?

_____
_____
_____
_____
_____
_____
_____
_____

Today I'm thankful for one or more of the following:

_____
Physical Provision

_____
Beautiful Person

_____
Special Blessing

Using the list of thanksgiving on the previous page, write out more details that explain what I can specifically thank God for.

_____
_____
_____
_____
_____
_____
_____
_____
_____

Pen A Prayer

_____
_____
_____
_____
_____
_____
_____
_____

Psalm 7:10-17   Day 2

Outlook

Thanksgiving is simply giving thanks.

Release and renew. What thoughts can I give to God so that thankfulness can be my focus?

_____
_____
_____
_____
_____
_____
_____
_____
_____

Today I'm thankful for one or more of the following:

_____
Physical Provision

_____
Beautiful Person

_____
Special Blessing

Write a list of adjectives (describing words) that would show my praise to God for his gracious gift of the provision, person or blessing I listed on the previous page.

_____
_____
_____
_____
_____
_____
_____

Pen A Prayer

_____
_____
_____
_____
_____
_____
_____
_____

Philippians 4:1-7

Day 3

Prayer

I want to take my requests to God with a thankful heart.

Confess and replace. What is in my heart that prevents me from being grateful to God?

_____
_____
_____
_____
_____
_____
_____
_____

Today I'm thankful for one or more of the following:

_____
Physical Provision

_____
Beautiful Person

_____
Special Blessing

Using the list of thanksgiving on the previous page, write out more details that explain what I can specifically thank God for.

_____
_____
_____
_____
_____
_____
_____
_____

Pen A Prayer

_____
_____
_____
_____
_____
_____
_____

We gather together to
ask the Lord's blessing;
He chastens and
hastens His will
to make known.
The wicked
oppressing
now cease from
distressing.
Sing praises
to His Name;
He forgets not His
own.
Edward Kremser

Psalm 9:1-9   Day 4

Focus

Recounting God's work in my life makes me wholehearted.

Release and renew. What thoughts can I give to God so that thankfulness can be my focus?

_____
_____
_____
_____
_____
_____
_____
_____

Today I'm thankful for one or more of the following:

_____
Physical Provision

_____
Beautiful Person

_____
Special Blessing

Write a list of adjectives (describing words) that would show my praise to God for his gracious gift of the provision, person or blessing I listed on the previous page.

_____
_____
_____
_____
_____
_____
_____

Pen A Prayer

_____
_____
_____
_____
_____
_____
_____

Psalm 145:1-10   **Day 5**

Goodness

Give thanks for God is good.

Confess and replace. What is in my heart that prevents me from being grateful to God?

_____
_____
_____
_____
_____
_____
_____
_____

Today I'm thankful for one or more of the following:

_____
Physical Provision

_____
Beautiful Person

_____
Special Blessing

Using the list of thanksgiving on the previous page, write out more details that explain what I can specifically thank God for.

_____
_____
_____
_____
_____
_____
_____
_____

Pen A Prayer

_____
_____
_____
_____
_____
_____
_____
_____

Psalm 105:1-7

Day 6

Publicize

What has God done in my life that I can tell someone about today?

Release and renew. What thoughts can I give to God so that thankfulness can be my focus?

_____
_____
_____
_____
_____
_____
_____
_____
_____

Today I'm thankful for one or more of the following:

_____
Physical Provision

_____
Beautiful Person

_____
Special Blessing

Write a list of adjectives (describing words) that would show my praise to God for his gracious gift of the provision, person or blessing I listed on the previous page.

_____
_____
_____
_____
_____
_____
_____

Pen A Prayer

_____
_____
_____
_____
_____
_____
_____

If the only prayer you said was thank you, that would be enough.
—Meister Eckhart

Psalm 95:1-6   Day 7

Expectant

Come into His presence with thanksgiving.

Confess and replace. What is in my heart that prevents me from being grateful to God?

_____
_____
_____
_____
_____
_____
_____
_____
_____

Today I'm thankful for one or more of the following:

_____
Physical Provision

_____
Beautiful Person

_____
Special Blessing

Using the list of thanksgiving on the previous page, write out more details that explain what I can specifically thank God for.

_____
_____
_____
_____
_____
_____
_____

Pen A Prayer

_____
_____
_____
_____
_____
_____
_____

Psalm 136:1-9   Day 8

Blessed

His steadfast love endures forever.

Release and renew. What thoughts can I give to God so that thankfulness can be my focus?

_____
_____
_____
_____
_____
_____
_____
_____

Today I'm thankful for one or more of the following:

_____
Physical Provision

_____
Beautiful Person

_____
Special Blessing

Write a list of adjectives (describing words) that would show my praise to God for his gracious gift of the provision, person or blessing I listed on the previous page.

_____
_____
_____
_____
_____
_____
_____
_____

Pen A Prayer

_____
_____
_____
_____
_____
_____
_____
_____
_____

Ephesians 5:15-21

Day 9

United

Thanksgiving is a standard to which I can align my words and actions.

Confess and replace. What is in my heart that prevents me from being grateful to God?

_____
_____
_____
_____
_____
_____
_____
_____

Today I'm thankful for one or more of the following:

_____
Physical Provision

_____
Beautiful Person

_____
Special Blessing

Using the list of thanksgiving on the previous page, write out more details that explain what I can specifically thank God for.

_____
_____
_____
_____
_____
_____
_____
_____

Pen A Prayer

_____
_____
_____
_____
_____
_____
_____
_____

Let us come into his presence with thanksgiving;
let us make a joyful noise to him with songs of praise!

Psalm 95:2

Psalm 107:1-9   **Day 10**

Delivered

Release and renew. What thoughts can I give to God so that thankfulness can be my focus?

I can always cry to the Lord in my distress.

_____
_____
_____
_____
_____
_____
_____
_____

Today I'm thankful for one or more of the following:

_____
Physical Provision

_____
Beautiful Person

_____
Special Blessing

Write a list of adjectives (describing words) that would show my praise to God for his gracious gift of the provision, person or blessing I listed on the previous page.

_____
_____
_____
_____
_____
_____
_____

Pen A Prayer

_____
_____
_____
_____
_____
_____
_____

*It is not
how much we have,
but how much we enjoy,
that makes happiness.*
– *Charles Spurgeon*

Psalm 107:10-21   Day 11

Wondrous

Confess and replace. What is in my heart that prevents me from being grateful to God?

May the Lord be praised for His works.

_____
_____
_____
_____
_____
_____
_____
_____

Today I'm thankful for one or more of the following:

_____
Physical Provision

_____
Beautiful Person

_____
Special Blessing

Using the list of thanksgiving on the previous page, write out more details that explain what I can specifically thank God for.

_____
_____
_____
_____
_____
_____
_____
_____

Pen A Prayer

_____
_____
_____
_____
_____
_____
_____
_____

Psalm 107:22-31　　　　　**Day 12**

Tell

Giving thanks is a willing sacrifice.

Release and renew. What thoughts can I give to God so that thankfulness can be my focus?

_____
_____
_____
_____
_____
_____
_____
_____
_____

Today I'm thankful for one or more of the following:

_____
Physical Provision

_____
Beautiful Person

_____
Special Blessing

Write a list of adjectives (describing words) that would show my praise to God for his gracious gift of the provision, person or blessing I listed on the previous page.

_____
_____
_____
_____
_____
_____
_____

Pen A Prayer

_____
_____
_____
_____
_____
_____
_____
_____

Psalm 100:1-5   Day 13

Presence

Confess and replace. What is in my heart that prevents me from being grateful to God?

Give God honor and glory for the power is His.

_____
_____
_____
_____
_____
_____
_____
_____

Today I'm thankful for one or more of the following:

_____
Physical Provision

_____
Beautiful Person

_____
Special Blessing

Using the list of thanksgiving on the previous page, write out more details that explain what I can specifically thank God for.

_____
_____
_____
_____
_____
_____
_____

Pen A Prayer

_____
_____
_____
_____
_____
_____
_____
_____

I will give thanks to you, LORD, with all my heart;
I will tell of all your wonderful deeds.
Psalm 9:1

1 Timothy 4:1-5

Day 14

All

Everything created by God is good.

Release and renew. What thoughts can I give to God so that thankfulness can be my focus?

_____
_____
_____
_____
_____
_____
_____
_____

Today I'm thankful for one or more of the following:

_____
Physical Provision

_____
Beautiful Person

_____
Special Blessing

Write a list of adjectives (describing words) that would show my praise to God for his gracious gift of the provision, person or blessing I listed on the previous page.

_____
_____
_____
_____
_____
_____
_____

Pen A Prayer

_____
_____
_____
_____
_____
_____
_____

Colossians 3:12-17   Day 15

Grateful

I want to do all for God's glory.

Confess and replace. What is in my heart that prevents me from being grateful to God?

_____
_____
_____
_____
_____
_____
_____
_____

Today I'm thankful for one or more of the following:

_____
Physical Provision

_____
Beautiful Person

_____
Special Blessing

Using the list of thanksgiving on the previous page, write out more details that explain what I can specifically thank God for.

_____
_____
_____
_____
_____
_____
_____
_____
_____

Pen A Prayer

_____
_____
_____
_____
_____
_____
_____
_____
_____

Isaiah 12:1-6   Day 16

Mercy

The Lord longs to
comfort me.

Release and renew.
What thoughts can I
give to God so that
thankfulness can be
my focus?

_____
_____
_____
_____
_____
_____
_____
_____
_____

Today I'm thankful for one or more of the following:

_____
Physical Provision

_____
Beautiful Person

_____
Special Blessing

Write a list of adjectives (describing words) that would show my praise to God for his gracious gift of the provision, person or blessing I listed on the previous page.

_____
_____
_____
_____
_____
_____
_____

Pen A Prayer

_____
_____
_____
_____
_____
_____
_____
_____

*It is in our acceptance
of what is given
that God gives Himself.*

– Elisabeth Elliot

Psalm 69:29-34   **Day 17**

Decision

When in pain, thanksgiving is a powerful tool.

Confess and replace. What is in my heart that prevents me from being grateful to God?

_____
_____
_____
_____
_____
_____
_____
_____

Today I'm thankful for one or more of the following:

_____
Physical Provision

_____
Beautiful Person

_____
Special Blessing

Using the list of thanksgiving on the previous page, write out more details that explain what I can specifically thank God for.

_____
_____
_____
_____
_____
_____
_____
_____

Pen A Prayer

_____
_____
_____
_____
_____
_____
_____
_____

Psalm 147:1-7　　　　　　　　Day 18

Sing

Thanksgiving creates a beautiful melody.

Release and renew. What thoughts can I give to God so that thankfulness can be my focus?

_____
_____
_____
_____
_____
_____
_____

Today I'm thankful for one or more of the following:

_____
Physical Provision

_____
Beautiful Person

_____
Special Blessing

Write a list of adjectives (describing words) that would show my praise to God for his gracious gift of the provision, person or blessing I listed on the previous page.

_____
_____
_____
_____
_____
_____
_____

Pen A Prayer

_____
_____
_____
_____
_____
_____
_____
_____
_____

Colossians 4:1-6

Day 19

Attentive

Look for ways to give God thanks.

Confess and replace. What is in my heart that prevents me from being grateful to God?

_____
_____
_____
_____
_____
_____
_____
_____

Today I'm thankful for one or more of the following:

_____
Physical Provision

_____
Beautiful Person

_____
Special Blessing

Using the list of thanksgiving on the previous page, write out more details that explain what I can specifically thank God for.

_____
_____
_____
_____
_____
_____
_____
_____

Pen A Prayer

_____
_____
_____
_____
_____
_____
_____
_____

Psalm 75:1-7 　　　　　　　　 Day 20

Rest

Relax and recount God's gifts.

Release and renew. What thoughts can I give to God so that thankfulness can be my focus?

_____
_____
_____
_____
_____
_____
_____
_____
_____

Today I'm thankful for one or more of the following:

_____
Physical Provision

_____
Beautiful Person

_____
Special Blessing

Write a list of adjectives (describing words) that would show my praise to God for his gracious gift of the provision, person or blessing I listed on the previous page.

_____
_____
_____
_____
_____
_____
_____
_____

Pen A Prayer

_____
_____
_____
_____
_____
_____
_____
_____

Psalm 30:1-12   Day 21

Redeemed

Lord, I'm so grateful for your redemptive work in my life.

Confess and replace. What is in my heart that prevents me from being grateful to God?

_____
_____
_____
_____
_____
_____
_____

Today I'm thankful for one or more of the following:

_____
Physical Provision

_____
Beautiful Person

_____
Special Blessing

Using the list of thanksgiving on the previous page, write out more details that explain what I can specifically thank God for.

_____
_____
_____
_____
_____
_____
_____
_____

Pen A Prayer

_____
_____
_____
_____
_____
_____
_____
_____

Gratitude will fertilize a strong mind; showing our thanks will cultivate serious growth.

—*Rachel Wojo,*
One More Step

Psalm 116:14-19

Day 22

Free

No bond of sin is too strong for the blood of Jesus.

Release and renew. What thoughts can I give to God so that thankfulness can be my focus?

_____
_____
_____
_____
_____
_____
_____
_____

Today I'm thankful for one or more of the following:

_____
Physical Provision

_____
Beautiful Person

_____
Special Blessing

Write a list of adjectives (describing words) that would show my praise to God for his gracious gift of the provision, person or blessing I listed on the previous page.

_____
_____
_____
_____
_____
_____
_____

Pen A Prayer

_____
_____
_____
_____
_____
_____
_____

1 Chronicles 16:27-34

Day 23

Attribute

Give the Lord the glory due to Him.

Confess and replace. What is in my heart that prevents me from being grateful to God?

_____
_____
_____
_____
_____
_____
_____
_____

Today I'm thankful for one or more of the following:

_____
Physical Provision

_____
Beautiful Person

_____
Special Blessing

Using the list of thanksgiving on the previous page, write out more details that explain what I can specifically thank God for.

Pen A Prayer

Even when I can't find thanks in my heart for what God is doing, I can always find praise for who he is.
-Rachel Wojo,
One More Step

Psalm 26:1-7　　　　　　　Day 24

Humble

May my heart be filled with gratitude for the hope I have in Christ.

Release and renew. What thoughts can I give to God so that thankfulness can be my focus?

_____
_____
_____
_____
_____
_____
_____
_____

Today I'm thankful for one or more of the following:

_____
Physical Provision

_____
Beautiful Person

_____
Special Blessing

Write a list of adjectives (describing words) that would show my praise to God for his gracious gift of the provision, person or blessing I listed on the previous page.

_____
_____
_____
_____
_____
_____
_____

Pen A Prayer

_____
_____
_____
_____
_____
_____
_____
_____

Psalm 28:1-7

Day 25

Strength

My soul must trust in Him alone.

Confess and replace. What is in my heart that prevents me from being grateful to God?

_____
_____
_____
_____
_____
_____
_____
_____

Today I'm thankful for one or more of the following:

_____
Physical Provision

_____
Beautiful Person

_____
Special Blessing

Using the list of thanksgiving on the previous page, write out more details that explain what I can specifically thank God for.

_____
_____
_____
_____
_____
_____
_____
_____

Pen A Prayer

_____
_____
_____
_____
_____
_____
_____
_____

The Lord is my strength and
my shield;
in him my heart trusts,
and I am helped;
my heart exults,
and with my song
I give thanks to him.

Psalm 28:7

Hebrews 12:22-29   Day 26

Anticipation

The shaking of this world makes way for a kingdom that cannot be shaken.

Release and renew. What thoughts can I give to God so that thankfulness can be my focus?

_____
_____
_____
_____
_____
_____
_____
_____

Today I'm thankful for one or more of the following:

_____
Physical Provision

_____
Beautiful Person

_____
Special Blessing

Write a list of adjectives (describing words) that would show my praise to God for his gracious gift of the provision, person or blessing I listed on the previous page.

_____
_____
_____
_____
_____
_____
_____
_____

Pen A Prayer

_____
_____
_____
_____
_____
_____
_____
_____
_____

1 Thessalonians 5:12-17

Day 27

Everything

Always give thanks for God's will.

Confess and replace. What is in my heart that prevents me from being grateful to God?

_____
_____
_____
_____
_____
_____
_____
_____

Today I'm thankful for one or more of the following:

_____
Physical Provision

_____
Beautiful Person

_____
Special Blessing

Using the list of thanksgiving on the previous page, write out more details that explain what I can specifically thank God for.

_____
_____
_____
_____
_____
_____
_____
_____

Pen A Prayer

_____
_____
_____
_____
_____
_____
_____
_____

Jeremiah 33:1-11

Day 28

Offering

I can always bring a thanks offering to the Lord.

Release and renew. What thoughts can I give to God so that thankfulness can be my focus?

_____
_____
_____
_____
_____
_____
_____
_____

Today I'm thankful for one or more of the following:

_____
Physical Provision

_____
Beautiful Person

_____
Special Blessing

Write a list of adjectives (describing words) that would show my praise to God for his gracious gift of the provision, person or blessing I listed on the previous page.

_____
_____
_____
_____
_____
_____
_____
_____

Pen A Prayer

_____
_____
_____
_____
_____
_____
_____
_____

Psalm 106:1-5

Day 29

Every

What can I praise God for right now?

Confess and replace. What is in my heart that prevents me from being grateful to God?

_____
_____
_____
_____
_____
_____
_____
_____

Today I'm thankful for one or more of the following:

_____
Physical Provision

_____
Beautiful Person

_____
Special Blessing

Using the list of thanksgiving on the previous page, write out more details that explain what I can specifically thank God for.

_____
_____
_____
_____
_____
_____
_____
_____

Pen A Prayer

_____
_____
_____
_____
_____
_____
_____
_____

Psalm 28:1-7   Day 30

Wisdom

The only power or strength I have comes from God.

Release and renew. What thoughts can I give to God so that thankfulness can be my focus?

_____
_____
_____
_____
_____
_____
_____

Today I'm thankful for one or more of the following:

_____
Physical Provision

_____
Beautiful Person

_____
Special Blessing

Write a list of adjectives (describing words) that would show my praise to God for his gracious gift of the provision, person or blessing I listed on the previous page.

_____
_____
_____
_____
_____
_____
_____
_____

Pen A Prayer

_____
_____
_____
_____
_____
_____
_____
_____

2 Corinthians 9:6-15

Day 31

Gift

I can always give thanks for grace.

Confess and replace. What is in my heart that prevents me from being grateful to God?

_____
_____
_____
_____
_____
_____
_____

Today I'm thankful for one or more of the following:

_____
Physical Provision

_____
Beautiful Person

_____
Special Blessing

Using the list of thanksgiving on the previous page, write out more details that explain what I can specifically thank God for.

_____
_____
_____
_____
_____
_____
_____
_____

Pen A Prayer

_____
_____
_____
_____
_____
_____
_____
_____

Put a Bow on It!

You did it! You read your Bible for 31 days in a row!

Throughout this month of Scripture reading, I've been reminded that life is rich when I am grateful. Giving out of a thankful heart enables living out a thankful heart. I have so enjoyed taking time to note my praise and thanks for all our God has done.

I pray that as you've walked this 31-day path, you've enjoyed the journaling methods and each one has spurred you on to cultivate a gratitude attitude like you've never had before.

May we continue to thank and praise our Lord for his mercy and grace.

Thanks for joining me on this journey through the Bible. Discover more Bible reading plans & journals at rachelwojo.com/shop.

Additional Notes

About the Author

Rachel "Wojo" Wojnarowski is wife to Matt and mom to seven wonderful kids. Her greatest passion is inspiring others to welcome Jesus into their lives and enjoy the abundant life he offers.

As a sought-after blogger and writer, she sees thousands of readers visit her blog daily. Rachel leads community ladies' Bible studies in central Ohio and serves as an event planner and speaker. In her "free time" she crochets, knits, and sews handmade clothing. Okay, not really. She enjoys running and she's a tech geek at heart.

Reader, writer, speaker, and dreamer, Rachel can be found on her website at www.RachelWojo.com.

Free Bible Study Video Series

If you enjoyed this Bible reading plan & journal, then you'll love Rachel's free video Bible study to help you find strength for difficult seasons of life! http://rachelwojo.com/free-bible-study-video-series-for-one-more-step/

Feel like giving up?

Are you ready to quit? Give up? But deep down, you want to figure out how to keep on keeping on?

Like you, Rachel has faced experiences that crushed her dreams of the perfect life: a failed marriage, a daughter's heartbreaking diagnosis, and more. In this book, she transparently shares her pain and empathizes with yours, then points you to the path of God's Word, where you'll find hope to carry you forward. One More Step gives you permission to ache freely—and helps you believe that life won't always be this hard. No matter the circumstances you face, through these pages you'll learn to...

- persevere through out-of-control circumstances and gain a more intimate relationship with Jesus
- run to God's Word when discouragement strikes
- replace feelings of despair with truths of Scripture

BUY NOW
www.rachelwojo.com/onemorestep

If you enjoyed this Bible reading plan and journal, then you'll love:

RACHEL WOJO — Pure Joy
cultivating a happy heart
BIBLE READING PLAN & JOURNAL

RACHEL WOJO — True Love
embracing the Father's affection
BIBLE READING PLAN & JOURNAL

RACHEL WOJO — Perfect Peace
starting my eyes on Jesus
BIBLE READING PLAN & JOURNAL

RACHEL WOJO — Confident Trust
believing God's plan is best
BIBLE READING PLAN & JOURNAL

RACHEL WOJO — Never Alone
remembering God is with me
BIBLE READING PLAN & JOURNAL

RACHEL WOJO — Soul Secure
winning over worry through God's Word
BIBLE READING PLAN & JOURNAL

RACHEL WOJO — Purposeful Pause
waiting on God's perfect timing
BIBLE READING PLAN & JOURNAL

RACHEL WOJO — Everything Beautiful
savoring God's seasonal elegance
BIBLE READING PLAN & JOURNAL

RACHEL WOJO — No Fear
choosing faith when I am afraid
BIBLE READING PLAN & JOURNAL

http://rachelwojo.com/shop

Made in the USA
Lexington, KY
26 October 2018